FIND YOUR COURAGE

How to think clearly and speak
common sense in a confused culture

VICKI L. RICH

Printed in the United States of America.

Cover and Interior Design: Bogdan Matei
Editor: Laurie Wilson

313 Publishing
6956 E. Broad St, #177
Columbus, OH 43213

TABLE OF CONTENTS

INTRODUCTION

I coach people. Not athletes, but leaders and career professionals seeking to reach their next level. Some coaches excel as high energy motivators. I tend instead to be known for calming the chaos and simplifying the complex.

That is part of what I want to do for you with this book. Do you sometimes feel unsettled by how confused and upside down our culture seems right now? Maybe you don't like to think about it because it's too much and you don't know where to start.

I want to help you clear your thoughts and determine where you stand on some controversial, but pervasive, cultural topics. My prior career was in politics. I enjoy reading, discussing and analyzing all things political.

I have read that more than 60% of Americans are afraid to share their beliefs because they might offend someone. Let us have a conversation about getting common sense and shared principles back into our public dialogue

The social activists are speaking everywhere: In our public offices, in the media, online, at workplace trainings, to our kids, and even in our churches. We cannot be silent while radicals wreak undue influence on our culture. We must find the courage to stand up and speak up when and where we find the need.

CHAPTER ONE

MAKE
POLITICS FUN

I've Liked Talking Politics for as Long as I Remember

An early childhood memory I have of my dad is being with him for an evening stroll. Well, Dad was on the stroll; I was tagging along. At our farm there was a long driveway that traveled from the house up a rolling hill for about 200 yards. Dad had stopped (for no reason that my child mind could find) to stand silently and gaze into the distance. I tried looking where his eyes aimed, and I saw nothing to study. I remember looking up at what was then his incredibly tall 6'4" frame next to my five-year-old shortness. I was momentarily silent, frozen in time by my curiosity about his stillness.

That didn't last long—my silence, I mean. I was not known as the quiet kid. Not me. I was the youngest of nine, most of whom were at least 10 years older than I. Our family gatherings were large and loud. And I reveled in the bustle. I remember talking and laughing and asking questions or telling stories whenever I felt like it—not only during those family parties, but any time I was around people.

Still and quiet were not yet states of being that I understood. In second grade, I was once sent to stand in the corner for humming in class. The teacher told

9

me to stay there until I stopped humming. It took a while. When I was that young, there were not many times when I wasn't either in motion or talking or both. I'm sure this was also true while my dad was standing there in some type of reflective time. The little person by his side was probably wiggling or shuffling and asking rapid-fire questions. He didn't chide me or tell me to stop, he just kept doing what he was doing.

I mostly remember the moment because I remember the image I saw when I looked up at Dad. He seemed tall and straight, still and steady, quiet and strong. I couldn't understand where he was looking, but it seemed to me that he was focused. And he certainly did not feel the need to explain himself to me.

That picture reminds me of how I saw my dad. He had a strength about him that suggested he knew who he was and what he believed in. He seemed steady and sure, not easily rattled. I felt safe and secure around him. He was a hard worker who believed in sacrifice for others more than frivolous gain for himself. He was also humble, and friendly to his peers; I remember countless friends and colleagues who seemed to enjoy talking and visiting with my dad. Much of this I observed from my vantage point as the disruptive noise maker in his midst, until I grew just a little bit older and began to want to talk to him more.

I respected both of my parents immensely from a young age. It was easy to see them as people who knew what they were talking about—largely because they lived how they said they believed. As I recall, if they said they would do something, then they did it. If they claimed something was important to them, then they lived like that something was important. How they lived was aligned with what they said. Even a little child could respond to that—genuine people make us comfortable. My parents were genuine.

I also intuitively saw my dad as smart, so I listened to him when he talked with others about the way things worked. At the feed store or local convenience store, I listened in as he talked with a couple of men about words I did not yet understand, like embargo, price-control and inflation. At home I later began my habit of watching the news with Dad. I listened in on Cronkite's anchor desk and reports from Donaldson and Rather, or morning chatter from Brokaw and Pauley. And then I would ask my dad questions or talk to him about what I thought.

My favorite topics were White House reports, presidential elections, and national political stories. I remember footage of the Convention floor where Reagan conceded to Ford, who went on to lose the fall election. I remember Dad's opposition to Tip O'Neill, both for his foreign policy positions and desire for universal government health care. I talked with Dad about the news topics and the responsibilities of presidents and Congress. And then I would go read books about America's founding to learn more—and bring my new knowledge back to the dinner table and talk more. By my early teens I was hooked. I developed a lifelong interest in politics there in the family room with my parents. I did not grow up on the rubber chicken dinner circuit watching my parents join in on local party politics—I simply learned about world and American history and was curious about current events. And I connected with my dad over conversations about those events from time to time.

That is why politics never was a frustrating topic for me. It started out as a simple relationship. I paid attention to the news and then became interested in learning more. Thanks to my fourth-grade social studies teacher, I also learned that the best way to learn history is to learn about people. He instilled in me a love of biographies—Alexander the Great, Benjamin Franklin. Daniel Boone, James Cash, Socrates. In getting to the know the people, I was also learning about the times in which they lived. When I began to learn politics and current events, I also was fascinated to learn what I could about the people and why they believed what they said they believed.

I hear many people use the word "politics" when they mean something negative, like jostling for power and money, or dodging responsibility and shifting blame. I know others that don't like to think about it at all and dismiss it as only related to government. "Politics" comes from the Greek word for city, though, and first referred to the public affairs of the city. I would personally translate that as affairs of the community—meaning our shared interests.

My understanding of politics is simple: Politics is the way a society organizes itself. As members of the society where we live, then, we each have a vested interest in the politics around us. In this nation, these United States of America, we also have a political system that allows for, and indeed calls for, active citizenship. We have opportunity here to be engaged citizens, not just engaged voters, but engaged voices and thought leaders who can shape how we organize our society. Tuning out politics is, in a way, also shaping our society.

I share the belief, along with many others, that there is a silent majority not speaking up in the current culture of increasing confusion. Meanwhile, activists and influencers are shaping opinions and legislation and narratives that have the potential to reshape significant aspects of our society. Some of those ideologies even contradict the foundational principles of our political framework—our shared citizen contract.

It is past time for more of us to speak up and speak clarity into these confusing and chaotic ideas that threaten to divide us more than they gather us. There are events occurring in our political and cultural midst that will affect our freedom of religion, our freedom of speech, our prosperity, our security, and our ability to get along with neighbors. I believe we are rising to levels where we are making choices on issues that are defining our cultural and political history. And it is important that we take notice and understand which choices we are making.

I encourage anyone who has some angst or concerns about our current cultural movements to pay attention to those concerns and decide where you stand. I recognize you may not like politics, but I encourage you to get beyond what you think about the word and focus instead on how you want your society to be shaped and organized. For me, the plumb lines (what I know to be straight and true and right) fall from two sources: my Christian faith and my United States heritage. These are baseline sources from which I form my understanding of how to live and of how to understand my role as an engaged citizen.

CHAPTER TWO

TRUST OUR HERITAGE

I shared already that I view politics as how we organize ourselves and prioritize our issues in society. How we go about doing that is under a framework or political system. In this nation, we have our foundational documents that guide us in how our government is structured, what our government's authority is, and how our government can operate in relation to its people.

There are three tenets, or foundational building blocks, that I consider deeply characteristic of our political framework and what our heritage means. Understanding these principles is the starting place for me in developing my personal positions on political issues or candidates. It does not mean there are no problems in our nation, or that our heritage is all rosiness and heroes. I don't know anyone who thinks that. But I will not knowingly vote against, or support movements that threaten, the tenets that I value in our heritage.

We Are a Nation of Laws, Founded on Ideas

We are founded on principled beliefs, concepts and ideas that were revolutionary in their time but had also been building over centuries. I believe that Mosaic Law, Greek and Roman politics, Classic Philosophy, Christian worldview, and the Enlightenment all influenced the minds and motives of the founding generation. Like the Magna Carta and its understanding that even the king was subject to the same laws, the Founders also believed that all government officials were equally governed by the laws of God just as any other citizen.

From their philosophies, legal, historical, and Christian-influenced education, they formed our structure to operate as a nation of laws. We are not a nation of men. We are not founded on bloodlines. We are not founded by cultural backgrounds or hierarchies. We are founded upon a system of laws and concepts and ideas. We have principles and founding documents that show us what that framework is. What we are founded on is that we agree in our heritage that we hold as our basic legal structure these concepts and ideas and laws—and that we will be governed by those principles and those laws. Rich and poor alike. Every ethnic background alike.

Now, I know there is debate. There is serious reflection and looking back over parts of our history where we did not live up to these ideals and standards. But the plumb line remains. The foundation and the principles are there for us to follow. They are there to guide us and challenge ourselves to live up to them. And that important tenet we must remember when we're considering all modern issues. Are we honoring our foundation and looking at this as though we are a nation of laws, or instead distracting ourselves by falling for movements that might make us a nation of collectivist interests where the individual is no longer sovereign? Where centralized power sources hold all property rights and distribute resources subjectively?

To keep our freedom and moral foundation, I believe we must remain a nation of laws and not men. When reform is needed, I favor policies that strengthen this tenet, not those that reject it.

We Hold Inalienable Rights

Another tenet of our political framework is this: We are a nation of independence. We were founded by people who understood and developed our principles around these ideas: That these truths are self-evident, and that all men are created equal. I have always understood this to be what is meant when people say American exceptionalism. It's not that we think we're exceptional because of geography, or because of who started our nation. We are not exceptional because of wealth or because of good things we have done. Our nation is exceptional in this way: Our founders understood that all men are equal because we are created equal. In other words, we are created with inherent value given naturally by a creator God. That is a unique principle upon which this country was founded.

Government did not grant our rights. Government does not grant our equality. Our government is to understand that we know as people that each one of us holds equal value in the eyes of something or someone much, much, much higher in authority than government. The Bill of Rights of the United States is not a set of benefits that the government gives its citizens. The Bill of Rights is instead a fence that we, the people, have put around ourselves; and that fence is a boundary that the government shall not cross. We have said, "We understand our rights as citizens and we understand our equal standing and equal value as citizens, and we are taking on the personal responsibility of governing our citizenry. And this is a boundary you, government, cannot cross. They are rights held within the people. They are rights naturally and God-given. They are not permissions that are granted. They are inalienable rights upon which you cannot encroach."

Power Is Limited by Balance

This is the rope that ties it all together and contains it so that it can work functionally under our core principles, even when things get complicated. The core concept under the balance of power tenet is that we govern best by maintaining a decentralized power structure. This is to prevent power from becoming too concentrated and in doing so become abusive and overbearing on its citizens.

I am sure you remember easily that the balance of power includes our three branches of government: Executive, Legislative and Judicial. These branches are equal and separate. There is another layer that balances out our power, one that is less talked about but just as important. That is the balance between the power given the federal government and the authority the state holds.

There is a desired tension between the local power and the national power. Those who govern closest to you are also those to whom you have the most access and ability to influence as a citizen. This decentralization of power that divides up the federal government into equal and separate branches; and maintains a tension between local authority verses distant authority is part of a design to keep power decentralized. We are a republic, from the Greek word meaning rights of citizens. The government structure was set up to operate of the people, by the people and for the people. Decentralized and balanced power is a part of that design.

Everyone principally operates off the same laws. And when we find that is not happening, we go back to the principle and follow the plumb line. That is the most practical way to resolve what is not working.

In summary, the three tenets I believe are key to ensuring we keep our political positions aligned with American heritage principles are these: We are a nation of laws. We are all inherently equal. Our government is limited by a decentralized balance of power.

Biblical Principles Give Deeper Understanding

I see many parallels between our American Heritage principles and biblical principles. I share this not to call the nation a Christian nation. The founders did not set up a theocratic system of government. They were, however, influenced by Christian principles. Some were Christian. Some were not. All borrowed from the laws of God, the laws of God's nature and the law of others before them who had followed God's laws in some way. The influences are undeniable.

For example, I see a biblical example when it came to establishing three branches of government. How did they decide what those branches or functions of government might be? In Isaiah 33:22 we are told "The LORD is our judge; the LORD is our lawgiver;

the LORD is our King." It is entirely reasonable to discern that since their education at the time included biblical heritage that they were influenced by its teachings.

Another biblical parallel seems evident in our concept of a justice system with balanced scales. We follow legal standards, not preferences and partiality. When it came to instructing His people how to judge fairly in their legal structure, God commanded them to be impartial. Leviticus 19:15 says "Do not pervert justice; do not show partiality to the poor or favoritism to the great; but judge your neighbor fairly."

Also, to understand our inalienable right of equality is to remember why every person has dignity—because we are all made in the image of God. Not every person chooses to follow God and become a child of God; but every human being is made in His image. As such all are created equal and hold inherent value or worth. Our foundational principles follow this spiritual truth and demand that our laws do as well. I am not more valuable than you because of a last name or any ancestry I may have; and you are not more valuable than I if your heritage or ancestry includes more traumatic events than mine. Everyone has equal value. It is our duty to honor that.

To understand how important decentralized, balanced power is to our sovereignty is to understand that centralized power is the beginning of tyranny. There is only one true King, and until He makes a new earth we will not have eternal peace. One day I believe every tear will be wiped away. Until that day comes, the promises of utopia—whether through centralized planning, artificial intelligence, technology, cultural Marxist revolution, or green salvation—are all false promises that will fall short. We must not devalue balance of power in favor of following those who say they know better than everyone and every being. It does not matter how benevolent the power seems at first; centralized earthly power will always lead to corruption and tyrannical control over subjects. This is just as true of socialism and oligarchical power as it is of fascism and authoritarianism.

Keep It Practical

I know it seems basic, but the beginning is a good place to start. And I do not only mean the founding of the national charters, but also the beginning of creation. As I have grown in my faith, I have learned a lot more about how all of the complex knowledge disciplines interact with or relate to each other in one way or another. In our advanced society, we are more and more reliant on experts in specific areas. This is a good thing, to abound in expertise. But it is also worth remembering that expertise in one discipline is not the sum-total of knowledge. The various knowledge disciplines do not exist in a vacuum or play by different natural laws or spiritual laws.

A political framework that denies the nature of property, posterity, or human nature toward reward for effort, for example, cannot work well. Human dignity, human sin, and the created order of the world will always be at play. That is, until Jesus returns.

Human nature is indeed why it is important to have laws. It is also why it's important to keep power in check. And, in my opinion, that means remembering why we were not founded to be underneath a heavy-handed government of central power.

The way I saw him, my dad had a right view of government. He was engaged intellectually on political ideas in his community and nation. He believed in staying aware. Yet he didn't look to government to run his life or propel his life. He looked to neighbors, family and his local community for his daily needs. Government and politics had his interest and his watchful eye; but did not play an outsized role in his life.

Politics loomed larger for me for much of my life, but only because I was interested in and employed in the field. I did react, though, when I found myself sitting across the desk from an employer who was telling me to "sit on" a regulation under my responsibility because she was passively punishing the group seeking its adoption. She did so because she didn't like their approach to lobbying. They had offended her, and she was using her power to hold the policy hostage as payback—even though we, too, were in favor of the same thing. It was a small thing, but it was also telling for me. I was not a part of the political party that usually believed unelected bureaucrats should have outsized power over citizens and industry. Everyone is susceptible to the use of power when given it—because of human nature.

Our foundational principles are simple...but not always easy to live by as a culture. So yes, more of us must be grounded in the basic principles so that we are more likely to preserve the ideas that matter. After all, it is way too easy to be distracted by the many messages that bombard us daily. It pays to be grounded first in what matters, so that we are more prepared to evaluate new information more easily. How do you filter your information for what is relevant to you?

CHAPTER THREE

DISCERN AS YOU LEARN

Know What You Stand For

Like I said, I like to follow political news. I enjoy following campaigns, and for most presidential campaigns I take the time to read candidates' positions and watch debaters and other events. I am typically not a low information voter, because of my general interest in politics, policy and campaigns. Many of my friends, however, are much less interested and cannot spend large amounts of time following candidates and issues.

It makes sense to me that my friends have lower interest in the details. I admit I am sometimes frustrated when they show no interest. This is especially true when I find them either unaware of what they support or actively supporting a candidate whose positions contradict values that my friends say are important to them.

I remember during the presidential campaign of 2020 when a Christian friend told me she could not vote for the president due to her faith. Because he had been adulterous in the past? No. It was because she thought he was rude and arrogant. That sounded to me more like an emotional reaction than a thoughtful response.

I didn't disagree with her assessment of the man. I asked though how she could vote at all if qualities like these disqualified him. It was not safe to put his opponent in a category of without sin. I would also argue that he too was rude and arrogant. He had a habit of challenging people on the campaign trail and had said some very questionable racial comments on more than one occasion.

Yet I did not wish to debate with her who had the worst personality. I cared more about the policies each promoted. I asked her if she had a problem with one of the president's specific positions or accomplishments. She expressed none. She did not seem to have awareness of what either candidate said he supported or wanted to do.

Then I asked if she had Christian concerns about the opponent's positions on a couple of specific things that I found harmful. Again, I was met with low interest. She did not seem to invest much energy in the issues themselves but was instead engaged in monitoring the personalities.

I had seen this many times before. If I learned one thing working on campaigns through the years, it was that many Americans maintain short attention and low interest to the issues candidates promote. We have that luxury, I suppose. We have just enough freedom, comfort and balance of power that we can ignore much of what those holding the seats of power do or say.

Such low awareness has been clear to me in recent years. When a president's administration tapped journalists' phones to spy on them in 2012, I do not recall any friends who expressed concern about endangering freedom of the press. Yet when a more recent president mocked the press and called them names, this was frightening to people I knew. I thought the scarier action was the one that involved spying on American journalists. It was not, however, as widely reported. People probably reacted less because it was promoted to them less.

I have also noticed people that seemingly vote in ways that contradict how they live. I have listened to friends share with me their personal convictions of forgiveness, personal responsibility, and even a desire to live a more holy life. Then I watched as some of those same people then supported candidates who promoted late-term abortion on demand, encouragement of irresponsible living, entitlement, and more; for no other voiced reason than inability to forgive a behavior or overlook a personality flaw.

I realized then that people sometimes support decisions for society in a much different way than they make decisions for themselves and their families. Many wish for their children to make wise choices and healthy choices; yet vote for policies that create incentives for making choices that cause personal hardship and heartache.

Some people, I am sure, do this knowingly. They believe in the actual policies and positions of the candidates they choose. They may believe that how they live their lives should be different than how they vote for society. They may even have reasons that I would understand and respect. I have friends who intentionally vote for policies I am opposed to, and I am grateful to live in a society where we can do so in staunch disagreement and still work and play together without a problem.

I fear, however, that this unity is slipping away. It is becoming more fragile in part because we, as a society, are drifting farther away from knowing the details and philosophy of our heritage. The more distant we become from a shared connection to that heritage, the more fragile our public debate will become.

I write also for those who, like me, have some angst about the propaganda that is overshadowing current cultural issues. How do we keep track of truth in a world of relativism? How do we choose what to research so that we can discern our personal positions on important matters?

Plenty of information is constantly at our fingertips. The problem is that quantity does not necessarily mean quality. Easy access to information doesn't even always save us time. Our time is precious, yet most of us willingly wade through mountains of information daily without ever filtering for relevance. Ironically, we don't have time to sort. It is a vicious cycle.

None of this information overload should be surprising to a person of faith. God has told us this would be our reality, that knowledge would increase, and people would run to and fro. If anything, we as Christians should know that as the world's birth pains increase, so will our technology and access to information.

The same Giver of Life who tells us of the future also gives us wisdom for discernment. Indeed, James tells us that God gives generously when we pray for wisdom. There are many ways He has shared that we may live wisely. One important way, as it relates to information overwhelm, is that we guard our hearts and understand what is truly in our hearts and minds at all times. . . for as go our hearts and minds also go our thoughts and actions. Another way we are guided about this is the warning to be careful and to fill our minds with what is good and true.

This is, in essence, where we begin when it comes to quickly and easily knowing where we stand on issues. We start from truth and view everything first through that lens. In a podcast I recently recorded, I called this following the plumb line instead of the fault line. We will stand stronger and think more quickly when we keep our focus on the plumb line . . . what is good and true. When we keep that marker in the foreground, we can keep the fault lines in the background where they are less able to distract us and deceive us. There is no need to give every message we hear or see the same weight and consideration.

Sort Information to Learn in Limited time

If you have ever been a student of marketing, then you've probably heard the adage that we buy on emotion and then justify our decision with logic. I am not an expert in sales, but I don't believe this means that we are in an irrational state when we buy. It is more about how we are motivated to act. We use our logic to gather and evaluate information and data. This gives us fodder to think. It is emotion, however, that prompts action. We use logic to determine the best product attributes. In the end though, we buy what we want. We do it when we have an emotion that motivates us to act.

I see some parallel here to understand sorting through information and focusing on what is useful and relevant. Too much information comes our way every day, even every minute, for all of it to capture our attention. Our eyes and minds are also continually filtering what we notice and what we do not. Marketers, news outlets and influencers know this. And they are all trying their best to use words and colors and pictures that will spark an emotion in you to evoke a response.

I suggest that maybe this is a good first step to evaluating where you will give your focus. It is not a bad thing that someone used emotion to catch your attention. But it is helpful for you to be aware if this was why something did. You may have noticed information on social media or in a political campaign because it sparked an emotion for you. Recognize that, and that those two sources of information are especially good at rousing emotional responses. But at this point, it is just information. Information is not the same thing as knowledge.

I will give an example from an emotionally charged topic. In April 2021, a police officer in my hometown area of Columbus, Ohio responded to a 9-1-1 call about an altercation involving someone wielding a knife. Because the news cycle works fast, the initial headlines, and even some of the rapid response stories gave few details. However, the timing of the incident was the same day that a verdict was coming down for the trial of the officer involved in the death of George Floyd. Emotions surrounding police interactions were likely running high for many writers and readers on that day.

One early headline simply said that a teenage girl was fatally shot by police. I remember another that said police shot and killed a teenager holding a knife. Additional headlines I noticed said similar things but added that the girl was black.

None of these headlines were inaccurate. They also did not provide knowledge—only information. If you read the headline only, you would have been left ignorant of what happened. The missing details mattered significantly.

Once I followed the story (or watched the body cam) for the remaining details, a much different picture came into focus. It was not a small altercation. There were several people on the scene when the officer arrived. One person was knocked to the ground and then violently kicked in the head right if front of the officer. At almost the same time, the girl wielding the knife had pinned another girl backward against a car and was about to stab her. Violently. She was not merely holding a knife, she had it raised high above her head and was about to plunge it into another person. The officer shot her to stop a probable attempted murder in progress.

I observed as some people reacted with emotion to the initial headlines as though they knew the whole story from those few words. There were a few public statements made that an unarmed person had been shot. Again, the headlines were not inaccurate (according to many media sources). Many media sources refer to "without a gun" as unarmed, even when they are knowingly speaking of someone who held other weapons. At worst, this is dishonest. At best it simply isn't telling the whole story. Some topics will evoke your emotions. Strong emotions can make us want to react quickly rather than respond with measure.

It is not that we need to stop and review every story in detail. Not everything will capture your interest in this way. It is OK to not learn more about every topic. I suggest though, to remember that information is not knowledge. Understand that just because you've heard or read one detail that caught your attention… it does not mean that you gained knowledge yet on that subject. Treat limited information as mere data—it is not a conclusion.

Seek Knowledge

We would ask too much of ourselves to attempt to follow every topic with high enough interest to build knowledge. There are some topics that will interest you more deeply than others. I recommend following those with intention; and allowing your brain to filter out the others much of the time. When it comes to news stories and current events, allow yourself the freedom to hold low information on the topics to which you cannot devote your time. The key is to learn to recognize that you have only collected information in those areas. Do not mistake emotional reaction as being the same thing as gaining knowledge on the matter.

I am not saying that I advocate running with low information on all topics. I encourage you to learn and grow on topics that fit your interests. I am merely advocating that you be honest with yourself about how much you can learn in a given time period. We simply cannot learn more than we can hold at a given time. We can, however, learn the basics and take seriously a responsibility to be informed citizens. More important, we can take seriously our responsibility to engage issues from a faith- and truth-centered worldview.

The most basic advice I have is to realize that much of what people share as knowledge is either not complete or also leaves room for other interpretations. It's not that people are deceiving you. It is that you too have knowledge. You may carry knowledge they do not have that allows you to understand things differently. Knowledge also is ever expanding. There is always more to learn.

As I mentioned, it is important to gain knowledge on the necessary things. In my earlier example, I would rather my friend choose something to learn about candidates when she votes. I do not think she needs to learn all the issues. There could, however, easily be one or two issues she could notice that would teach her more about what types of things the candidate will promote and support in office.

I have some suggestions for how to survey abundant information and choose areas where you see a need or have an interest in learning more. There are five things I look for to help me identify areas where I want to learn more in order to understand what I think about a particular topic.

- **Look for Patterns:** One tip is to search for patterns. There is a saying in self-improvement that the way we do one thing is the way we do most things. The way I understand this concept is that, for example, a person who lacks the ability to be disciplined in one area of life also does in other areas. It may show up as poor eating habits, no time for exercise, poor budgeting, etc. Varying areas are affected across differing functions. The same pattern, however, may be the common cause.

When it comes to quickly understanding divergent subject matters, I look for patterns in a similar way. There are patterns in nature, in business, in human nature, and in relationships. Our brains naturally seek out patterns when filtering through information. This can lead to error if we blindly follow a pattern or allow assumptions to make us see something from only one perspective.

Patterns, like information, are not knowledge. They are markers that guide me in what to investigate further if needed. Take my political candidate example: I may not know (or care) what a candidate's position is on every issue. I can know, however, whether he or she has a pattern of favoring centralized federal power or not. From there I then learn more about what it shows me about that person's positions and decision-making.

- **Look for parallels.** For areas where I have less knowledge, I have learned to apply parallel knowledge as a shortcut to determine how best to learn more. You probably do this all the time. For example, you may not know anything about how to grow a crop of corn. However, you may know how to grow flowers. There is parallel expertise here that you could apply, and then you'd see where you need to learn more.

- **Find incongruencies.** When an issue seems to be labeled or presented as something different than it functions, I take notice and spend time learning more. An example is when terms like "family planning" are used to support abortion. It strikes me as incongruent (and intentionally crafted) to say "family planning" when one is talking about preventing life that has already been conceived. When I see incongruent terms, it alerts me to learn more about what is being presented.

- **Seek Alignment.** You already have a baseline of knowledge. Look first to where new information aligns and where it does not. This gives you a marker for where you may need to evaluate what you think you know— to become skeptical of something that does not align with what you know to be true. Be open to learning that you are wrong. Be equally open to trusting truths that are already known. Seek the alignment.

- **Follow Inspiration.** This one is my personal preference. I would rather invest my energy and support in what is inspirational. I am more interested in human flourishing, for example, than constricting innovation and liberty. I am not as easily drawn to ideas and issues that are centered on tearing down or deconstructing.

The underlying key to all these tips, and to keep myself from feeling overwhelmed is this: The issue may be complex, but principles are not complicated. Follow the principles.

In the first chapter I wrote about some of the biblical and Constitutional principles that I stay grounded in to help me evaluate how I think about various issues. These principles do not instruct me specifically what to conclude about each issue. You and I may follow the same principle and be on a different side of any given issue. This is the beauty of both our political structure and of the gifts that God has given us.

We have differing interests, different expertise, varying preferences, and a whole host of perspectives that would lead us to divergent solutions even when operating under the same principles. Much like diverse opinions and thought make stronger and smarter teams, our culture becomes more vibrant due to a variety of ideas.

In the next few chapters I want to raise awareness about a different possibility: that there are advocates and cultural leaders advancing different kinds of principles. We know that not everyone holds the same worldview. And as people of faith, we also know that not every worldview is anchored in what is good and true and right. This is just a reality of a fallen world.

Have you given thought to how your personal values drive your views on issues? There are a few values I find particularly interesting in terms of how I believe they influence the way we show up in our political views. Can you guess what they may be?

CHAPTER FOUR

EMBRACE YOUR VALUES

Freedom, Liberty and Autonomy

When I work with clients to help them identify their top values, there is no question that freedom is a common value considered. Freedom comes to mind quickly for many of us. I think there are a few reasons for that. An obvious possibility is that we live in a nation known for freedom, and where our citizens have a general expectation to live as free people. It is a part of our national identity to recognize ourselves as free.

Another reason for attraction to freedom may stem from the free will we have been given. God created us with the freedom to make choices. Our choices are not limitless, however. We cannot choose beyond our natural realities. I can choose to learn to play basketball. I cannot, however, choose to be two feet taller. The freedom of my free will is limited by the laws of nature.

Free will also leads to consequences of choices. Every choice has a consequence. Some consequences go unnoticed, but they exist, nonetheless. Exercising a freedom to work a more flexible schedule may give me more time with family. That is a good consequence. Perhaps at the same time it costs me less interaction with my co-workers, and I then must make more choices to proactively stay engaged with them.

These limitations on free will—natural law constraints and consequences of our choices—point us to a spiritual truth about freedom. We reap what we sow, and we cannot mock God or His natural order (Galatians 6:7-8). In freedom we have an ability to make choices, but we are also called to be responsible and accountable for the choices we make. If we treat freedom as license to simply follow every desire, we invite decay and destruction. We find freedom's best consequences while sowing a life of obedience and honor to God in gratitude for His gift of eternal life.

I think, therefore, that we are naturally attracted to a value of freedom because we have an innate drive to be free, to make choices for ourselves. Sometimes disappointing circumstances lead my clients to temporarily place a high priority on freedom. Examples are those who were making career changes or leaving toxic workplaces. They sought to leave behind situations that confined them or bound them in some way. This made freedom a high priority for a season.

For some people there is a more lasting value that corresponds to a strong internal drive to create personal freedom. They are not only circumstantially driven to gain freedom from something, but also to find personal satisfaction in holding themselves responsible for the choices they make in life. For them it is worth the effort it takes to make wiser decisions, create habits, build discipline, assume risk, and correct course when necessary. They understand freedom as something more than a desire, but as an exercise of free will and personal responsibility that brings consequences they must also accept.

Freedom, when understood this way, is a value that Christians can also understand as having a moral obligation to God. We are not free to do whatever we want. That would be giving in to or living according to our sinful nature. Also, natural order of things prevents us from imagining or thinking our way to new realities. Freedom is not licentiousness or wild abandon. Freedom, rightly valued, is anchored in adherence to moral standards and personal responsibility.

We know these things to be true when we consider external examples: A free man may sacrifice his freedoms after committing murder, because society will restrain him for public safety. A person unwilling to discipline herself to eat healthy and exercise regularly will not enjoy the freedoms of a fit and energetic body. Freedom does not include one person's right to steal another person's freedom through bondage, for this is morally depraved.

Freedom is not unchecked pursuit of our desires. Freedom is our ability to make choices through the exercise of our free will. To value freedom means to also understand and accept responsibility for those choices.

Liberty

Our forefathers seemed to clearly view true freedom as bound by moral obligation to a higher power. I do not know what else to conclude when they wrote not only that we are created equal, but also that it should be self-evident that we are. In that one statement they testified that there is a higher power, that such a power created us, and that as such we all hold inherent and equal value.

It is naturally understood, then, that any higher power who created us would also be the ultimate moral authority. This implies to me that the Founding Fathers believed that natural law and moral standards are above us and above government, and instead begin with the ultimate authority or lawgiver. We cannot individually choose our own truths or morals; we must instead come to learn and understand what those are.

The Continental Congress had a similar understanding about liberty, I believe, that with liberty comes an obligation to abide by moral standards. While freedom generally refers to our personal values, liberty refers to our relationship with society and political structure. I think of it this way – we are born with our free will freedom. Liberty we may have to defend against or define for external forces.

Our founders understood us to be given by God both our right to life and our right to liberty. They were separating from a political structure where government granted liberties to its citizens as it desired. In our founding, however, it was established that there are rights we hold given to us not by government but given by God. Instead of the government granting us liberties, our structure was formed so that only through the consent of the people could government restrain our natural liberty. The Bill of Rights then did not define specific liberties granted by government but instead is a list of liberties people hold that government was not given authority to encroach upon.

This is an important understanding of liberty for United States citizens to realize. The emphasis of our liberty was freedom and independence, both of which placed personal responsibility and moral obligations at the feet of every citizen. It is famously claimed that John Adams said, "Our Constitution was made only for a moral and religious people. It is wholly inadequate to the government of any other."

To value liberty as a citizen, then, bears the same weight of personal responsibility as does freedom. To truly value liberty demands that we value others and treat them with dignity.

Autonomy

Autonomy as a personal value is easy to conflate with freedom. It is similar, but not quite the same. Autonomy is about self-directing and making our own decisions. In his book, *Drive*, Daniel Pink identifies autonomy as one of the top three elements required for employee motivation. He describes it as in our nature to want to self-direct (Pink, p. 87).

Pink's idea certainly resonates with me. In my career, I have sought autonomy in both my career decisions and in the way I performed my work functions. I am not a micromanager as a leader and tend to resist micromanagement when I can. Few things are more stifling to me than for someone to insist I do things a certain way or mire me in processes unnecessarily.

As a Christian, I now understand something about autonomy that I did not know years ago. Autonomy, like many things, is a good and helpful value in balance. It can, however, be taken to extremes and perhaps become unhealthy. This especially seems true as it relates to political or societal outcomes.

Self-directing is a good thing so long as it is about motivation, self-reliance and initiative to get things done. Much like freedom requires personal responsibility, autonomy has a necessary limiter or balancer as well. I believe that counterweight is humility, or something similar. Let me explain.

Self-direction left unchecked can become something that seems more like hedonism or a desire to self-create and be godlike. Hear why I say this: Just as overzealous self-direction at work could lead to choosing to aim for different goals than given—in life it could lead to imagining the power to disregard natural laws and consequences.

Autonomy run wild seems to lead to expectations that one can continually reinvent oneself according to various desires, and the state or society around them can adjust to those desires, or even erase consequences or outcomes. An example is a woman's expectation that her lifestyle ambitions give her license to end a life created by her previous choices so that she is not required to live out the consequences. Another example might be the expectation that a person self-direct by reinventing oneself by identifying as a different gender, or no gender, or several genders.

In either of these scenarios, an extreme example might be that the person has an expectation that the state should subsidize or provide any medicinal, procedural or mental health support required. At this stage, autonomy has risen to an arrogance that natural law can be ignored and society must bend to the person's direction. Autonomy taken too far then may impose burdens on or threaten liberty and freedom of society at large.

Joy or Ingratitude

Which perspective governs your life? When my mom was in hospice care dying of cancer, I was moved by the grace with which she was departing the world. Testament to the impression she was leaving on others at the same time came in the many notes and comments from nurses and caregivers. There were the usual pleasantries about how wonderful it was to know her—and there were multiple stories of how she had cared for them through counsel or gracious words in times of need.

Until walking through this season with her, I had not known how much grace my mom had. As I watched her and listened to her, I realized that Mom could die with such grace because she was perfectly content. Her contentment was so complete and so thorough, that I wanted to gather it in so that I could grow in strength and wisdom from her example. She was content with her life because she was grateful for her life—all of it—blessings and hardships alike.

It seemed she knew life itself to be a gift, as were all the people in her life. Mom's people were her family--the husband who had passed away already, and her nine children. She was grateful for her family and the time she had been given on this earth to love. Because she held such gratitude, it was her nature to be content and have an outlook of joy. And because of that, she found it easy to notice other people and really see them. I believe that is why she spent such quality time with her caregivers even though her own health was waning.

A joyful person usually seems content, would you agree? I've also found that when I'm around a person of joy, it is contagious. As my experience with Mom showed me, joy does not always include high energy and laughter. Joy is not mere happiness or happy feelings. Joy runs much, much deeper. Joy is a way of looking at life—a way of choosing to be positive and happy and content. For Mom, I learned that it came from gratitude. Because she remembered to be grateful throughout her life, she was content and had lasting joy.

I think Mom's example was the first time I realized how to develop joy. Before I had probably thought it to be an outcome of favorable circumstances or experiences. Mom showed me something more important: Joy is a choice. It is a state we can grow within ourselves by choosing to be grateful for life every day.

You may be wondering why I mention joy in relation to cultural and political issues. It may be obvious: You cannot be joyful and ungrateful at the same time. An attitude of ingratitude is counter to a state of joy. When you wallow in grievances, complaints, victimhood, disappointments, and bitterness; you rob yourself joy. Remember that our time is limited, and our lifespan is finite. Every hour spent with ingratitude reduces an hour or more of joy in life.

Another way I am thinking about this, in relation to some of today's cultural phenomena, is that joyful people do not seem enraged and bitter. Meanwhile those who look around their world and choose not to focus on reasons to be grateful—these are the people that miss out on joy and instead let ingratitude drive their disposition. This happens when we let circumstances drive how we feel, and then let how we feel drive our perspective and behaviors and lessen our self-regulation. Joy is an important anchor value to evaluate complex issues from a right perspective, and gratitude is a key ingredient to practice.

These are a few values that potentially play a big part of your understanding of political and cultural issues. You may have others that come to mind for you. Whatever they are, take some time to reflect on them and consider how they influence your thought patterns.

Sometimes political messages sock your emotions by appealing to or threatening your values. This can happen genuinely. For example, there may be a campaign to restrict rights that you value.

There are times, though, when political messages employ deception. I share more about this in the next chapter.

CHAPTER FIVE

DO NOT BE
DECEIVED

Now is a time for more conversations and thinking grounded in principles and reality. We hear a lot of talk from all corners abut following our values. Indeed, we often hear of two people on opposite sides of a political issue claiming that each position is an expression of American values. Why is that?

Frankly, I believe it is partly because a value is not as stable as a principle; it doesn't have the same consistency over time. Principles are more likely to stay in place . . . to follow a plumb line.

Thomas Jefferson said, "In matters of style, swim with the current and in matters of principle, stand like a rock."

Values not only vary among people; they change within a person over time or in different scenarios. Your granddad, for example, probably held a strong American value to respect the service of people like police. Meanwhile, a recent short-term football player became famous for wearing socks calling police pigs and parroting the phrase "fry them like bacon." His values are different from your grandfather's, but he would probably call them American.

A principle runs deeper and holds longer because it has more weight. This might help--think of it like a conviction. A mentor of mine has a saying that paints a picture well. He says values are what you care about, convictions are what you would sacrifice for.

A principle has that kind of weight . . . and it has objective clarity that endures.

Freedom of Speech is more than an American value, for example. It is a principle. It is baked right into the Bill of Rights even . . . right at the top. It has definition. It has meaning. Legal meaning. And it does not really matter if, say, radical students on college campuses value protection from offensive ideas more than free speech. The principle still stands, right in place like a plumb line, somewhere between their values of shutting down foul opinions and another radical's value of freedom to be obscene or harmful.

And that brings me to another American principle that still stands even though activists are doing their best to tear it down with wordplay and cultural deconstruction. Equality is a principle identified in our Declaration of Independence. We are created equal by God and are treated equal under the law. This is our ideal.

Radical leftists have something else in mind . . . something with a bigger reach but far less value in terms of quality of life, justice, and fairness. Their term is equity. To the average ear, on the head of someone with no political agenda, this can sound almost like the same thing. I think many people tend to hear equality when they say equity.

How does the equity movement differ from principles of equality? Does that difference matter to how we respond and what we do next?

Equality as a principle of our nation has a definition and a scope. We were founded with a principle that we as a nation, in our governmental, legal and policy structure will operate under the shared understanding that all people are to be treated equally under that law. We have not always hit the mark, but we did draw the plumb line from the start . . .and in doing so we made the mark visible and measurable. Because we took the effort to agree on that as a basic principle, our citizenry, our government entities and our courts have that plumb line by which to measure our policies and actions. It gives us a place of redress for where we can go when the standard is not met. When it was found to be true that people were not given equal access to a public venue, for example, it was the agreed-upon principle of every person being equal under the law that created a standard under which that inequality could be addressed. This is such a common understanding among our populace that we can easily brush past it and not give much thought to what equality means. But it does have meaning, and that meaning gives us common ground.

What is meant by equity? I found a clue from the National Academy of Public Administration. They call equity the fair, just and equitable management of all institutions serving the public; the fair, just and equitable distribution of public services and implementation of public policy; and the commitment to promote fairness, justice, and equity in the formation of public policy.

Seems harmless right? It seems from this definition that equity is not the principle; but is rather a means or method to reach a desired state (equal outcomes). That is why you'll hear the phrase "equality of outcomes."

Our founding principle, again, is that we are all equal in value already, and that our legal justice and political system should treat us that way. The equity movement changes this a bit by promoting an underlying viewpoint that if inequity exists in any from, then so does inequality. In other words, their philosophy is that if there is inequity, then there are people being treated unequally under the law. The solution then becomes to require equality of outcomes, or equity.

Sometimes it seems reasonable to make adjustments that even up the outcomes. For example, making buildings accessible to those with wheelchairs makes sense to most. I am not sure I would go so far as saying it makes access equitable. People with wheelchairs still have the same condition in relation to ability to walk as they originally had. To me, the building accommodation is still about equality... treating everyone with equal dignity and equal value may at times mean offering a hand up to some.

Equity as a political movement, however, is making a different statement. People promoting equity insist that all inequities must be corrected, even to the extent of holding others back or redistributing resources if necessary. Doing that, however, can become at odds with our principles of equality. If equity requires discrimination, after all, does it not demand inequality?

Issues can easily become complex. Principles, however, are simple. If policies on equity require moving away from our founding principles, then we as citizens need to take the time to think through clearly whether this is what we want. We must make sure we know what we are supporting or allowing to happen in our midst.

There is a meme on equity I have seen a few times on social media. The picture shows three people standing on boxes to peer over a fence watching a ball game. All the boxes are the same height, but each person is a different height. The tall person stands well above the fence while the shortest person cannot see over the fence at all. There is a corresponding picture next to this one, where a box is taken away from the tallest person and given to the shortest person so that everyone can see. That picture is labeled "equity."

Friends of mine have shared this meme and supported its conclusion. Admittedly, my first thought was that it is a poor example to use the idea of "stealing" the game at the fence while the background shows people in the stadium who paid to watch the game. Why should those people be treated unfairly by giving the people at the fence easier access to steal a free show?

Of course, a fair retort might be that the whole point is that not everyone can afford a ticket. I understand empathy about that. I would like to go to a Steeler's game but will probably never spend what it costs to do so. That does not mean anyone owes me an opportunity to go to one for free.

I digress. Perhaps the people in the background were also watching the game for free and the people at the fence simply wanted to be at the fence. If they simply made the choice to be there, then I have the same question: Why does their choice to be at the fence rather than inside require that they be given more (more boxes) so that they can watch? The meme again seems like a poor illustration to me. Even if the people needed to watch the game there and one needed a boost to see it, that does not mean that the only conclusion to have is that public policy should redistribute boxes (wealth) to achieve equity. In fact, I would argue that taking the box away from one to give to the other is simply a form if unequal treatment (dare I say stealing?). Or, if the one person gave up the box willingly to the other, then that is simply sharing.

What do our leaders say about equity? The current vice president told us in a previous political ad about equity. In it, she said "equality suggests that everyone should get the same amount. But the problem with that, not everybody's starting out from the same place." She ends up saying that if people start out at different places but are given equal amounts, there will still be disparate outcomes. She then says, "Equitable treatment means we all end up at that same place." (Harris, 2020)

This ad misrepresents the principle of equality. Equality is about fairness and treating people with dignity. Moreover, it shows a naïve understanding of outcomes and inequalities. It makes a presumption that redistributing resources will make it possible to make everything level and equitable, but that assumes people will not have free will and will not make choices they want to make.

For example, when we were kids headed to the county fair one day, my brother and I each were given $20 to spend. I spent all mine that day on games, rides and soda. He spent $5 and saved $15. We were given the same amount but ended our day with unequal amounts. Here is the kicker: If I'd been given more, I would have spent more. Saving that money was not going to be my option that day over experiencing fun at the fair. My choices and my consequences had an impact on my outcomes. Other factors will impact outcomes too. It is not all about distribution.

There is a bigger problem with the equity mindset. To get the outcome promoted in that political ad—to distribute resources to try to make everyone end up at the same place--requires the opposite of equal treatment. You will have to treat people unequally . . . give some more money, some more time, some unearned entry into jobs or other programs. You also, by the way, may have to treat them differently for their behavior (disregard justice). Some activists said as much during the protests and riots of 2020.

Social Justice isn't Justice

Chicago organizer Ariel Atkins told media outlets that her group 100% supported the violent looters who trashed large chunks of the city. She said it was "reparations". She said they should take what they want because businesses have insurance. That is not even the worst example of what I have heard from those who say that any means necessary is worth it to achieve their desired outcome of equity. It seems then that equity not only calls for redistribution and inequality, it also can call for illegal behavior and treating others unjustly.

And where does that leave us? Equality is a principle. Equality gives a measurable standard to guide us.

Equity is much more like a method than guidance. It doesn't give measurement to follow but instead needs to be measured. It does not seem to be a moral standard. Its moral quality is dependent on the moral qualities of those measuring or promoting it. And it seems to require partiality, to show favor to and give preferences to people according to subjective standards. This should perhaps give Christians pause. Partiality in justice is a problem for us.

How you view justice may have great impact on which issues are attractive to you. If you share a Christian worldview, I encourage you to take the necessary time to understand what your worldview teaches you about what justice is. In my view, many of the current cultural representations of justice not only pivot away from our constitutional framework; but many also teach justice as something contradictory to biblical justice.

In its simplest form biblical justice is impartial. Thaddeus Williamson, in his book, *Confronting Injustice without Compromising Truth*, also explains justice as giving people what they are due. This would include both giving God what is due, as well as giving the penalty due for any sin or crime. I put all this together to understand a couple things about justice. One is that biblical justice would demand that no person should be given preference or treated more harshly. A second is that while we may think we want justice, it is also humbling to remember that if God gives us what we are actually due, me may not like it much.

I am interested in thinking about this practically, at the intersections where public policy and culture interact. If justice is fairness and impartiality—it refers to giving to people what is due---then I believe that many things I hear described as social justice policies are not driven by justice. Yes, yes, I know many churches refer to social justice. I do not think most churches mean the same thing as do the social justice cultural activists. Much of what is promoted politically as social justice centers on redistribution; and the goal often is more about creating winners and losers or garnering voter support than it is about balancing the scales of justice.

In Leviticus and Deuteronomy we see that punishment should fit the crime and not be excessive to the crime. Everyone who comes before a court should be treated equally, not given special treatment for being poor or being from a different tribe.

There is something else about biblical justice that is important. Justice is fairness. This is not the same thing as "sameness." Remember the parable in Matthew 20 of the farmer who hired day laborers? People hired in the morning agreed to work the day for a denarius. Three more times in the day he went out and hired more workers, and no matter what time the workers started, each received a denarius at the end of the day.

When the morning workers saw the later arrivals were paid the same amount, they grumbled about unfairness. But the farmer rebuked them, for he had paid them what they had agreed was good pay. His agreement with others was none of their concern, nor was his decision about how to use his own money. The farmer, by the way, in this parable represented God. It would seem to me that God does not consider fairness as equal to sameness (or equity). They received the same amount through generosity, but they did not put in the same hours.

The laborers were all paid what they were due. That was just. The farmer was generous with those who had missed most the day's work. He was generous in caring for the needs of those who had less. That, too, was just. God's view of justice does indeed include loving our neighbors and caring for "the least of these."

What God's view of justice does not seem to allow are partiality (oppression OR favoritism), unfair penalty, vengeance, or pulling some down to give to others. Justice is not some subjective tug- of-war game where power or wealth are shifted to the winning side. Justice is not something we can measure in relationship to each other or by our perceptions of equity with others. Justice measures against an unchanging standard.

In our political system the standards are defined by our Constitutional principles and a law meant to be equally applied. The ultimate standard, however, is God's moral law. Justice means aligning with that standard. Much of what is advocated in the social justice movement not only disregards the presence of God's moral standards, but many solutions it calls for would instead create injustices.

If social justice appeals to you, it is probably because you desire justice. Give some thought to what your principles and biblical understanding inform you about what justice means. Get clear on that for yourself. Do not assume others believe the same thing. The social justice literature and activist leaders promote many ideas contrary to justice—in other words, immoral ideas. The term is deceiving because different belief systems motivate them (more on that in chapter seven). Discern what they mean before you support them.

Similarly, when leaders say "equity", do not automatically hear equality. Political leaders are using the word "equity" with intention. It is not a synonym. Principles like equality are extremely important right now. There are several areas where our fundamental rights as citizens, and our Christian principles, are under threat.

Now is not the time to tune out . . . and it is not the time to keep your story and your voice silent. Even young children are now taught some heart-breaking ideas about justice and racial attitudes. Some of these ideas go beyond deception and misleading terms. They are damaging and wicked. In the next chapter I will dive into a cultural movement I see as steeped in wickedness and driven by lies.

CHAPTER SIX

REJECT WICKEDNESS

Years ago, I campaigned for George W Bush's presidential run; I later worked in his administration. I had been a supporter since before he officially entered the race. I liked his style, his gubernatorial positions, and much of his message. One policy area I supported was his message of ensuring access to quality education for everyone. I particularly agreed that no child should be left behind and that soft bigotry of low expectations was one major barrier for young people. We shouldn't write anyone off as less than capable and expect for them less than every potential they can muster. I supported the issue because I believe in believing in people. I also believe that learning sparks potential and creates opportunity. And I wholeheartedly believe that we are all created equal and each therefore have unique gifts to bring to the world. These beliefs about equality and potential are what inspired me to support President Bush's messages on education. I later realized that federal bureaucracy would show a special capability for messing up inspiring ideas, but the original inspiration remains real for me: soft bigotry of low expectations thwarts promise and diminishes people.

That perspective is possibly why the concept of antiracism seemed shifty to me from the first moment

I heard it. I had heard someone on a podcast sharing about some trainings on diversity and inclusion. The speaker was promoting a couple books and conveyed that all white people are born inherently racist, and that black people are an oppressed group held under by the systemically racist white hierarchy. Her message also included things about the need to be actively antiracist; and she suggested everyone read from a list of books to learn about systemic racism and white oppression.

It didn't pass the smell test from the get-go. To me, it seemed ridiculous for her to even be saying out loud that all black people are this and all white people are that. Could she not hear the racism in her own words? Or the lack of humanity in reducing people to nothing more than a classification by skin color or group iden-tity? We had just blown past soft bigotry. This sounded like big-league, hard-as-nails bigotry.

I detested what I heard, and a part of me scoffed at it with intention to write it off as nonsense that would gain no traction. Yet there was also a part of me that became curious. It was like car crash debris on the side of the road. I could not help but stare--even though I knew I might be looking at pain and suffering.

I began reading the recommended books, start-ing with a pop culture book on fragility. It did not add depth to the subject. I moved on next to a book defining antiracism. At least then I was learning what movement leaders believed on the topic. I think I was about half-way through that book when I started to learn this was not an isolated fad. The country was about to erupt in this national group think discussion defining almost every walk of life in terms of white people against black people or vice versa. It seemed as though diversity had become an idol instead of a goal, and that culture was determined to divide people while unironically touting that division as a path to unity. Who would believe in these things?

I soon learned an answer. A close friend invited me to a webinar to hear a white influencer as he coached other white people to believe they may be racist. He was not an expert on the topic, by the way, but was trying to sell a group mastermind so that he too could make money off the topic.

Another friend shared that he was in a corporate training that had sectioned white people from black people. I have no idea where that left people of neither group. I had read articles about such trainings happening in local and federal government agencies, where white employees were instructed to denounce their "whiteness." How is this something that any employer would see as team building?

But there was more. I was shocked to hear from my sister that a national publication in her church was promoting antiracism bigotry. It seemed surreal. How could anyone with a Christian worldview promote divisiveness like labeling people by skin color? It turns out though, that the church is not immune to secular cultural influences. I personally heard a pastoral influencer, a person of impeccable credibility, say that all white people are inherently racist. It was his emotional reaction to a national current event. I am not sure if or how his opinion evolved after that.

Other church leaders have doubled down on divisive partiality in the name of dismantling racial bias.

One major denomination is training pastors and lay-people alike that whiteness is itself racism and that black bigotry can never be racism. Do you hear the sinful ring to this?

It is pervasive. And while some people are just quietly tolerating it for fear of rebuke, others are taking it as truth because they hear it from all corners. I challenge each of us, especially those of us who are Christian, to resist each of these approaches. We cannot stay silent in the face of sinful and hateful teaching. We also cannot be passively gullible when worldly passions are preached from the pulpit.

An Ideology of Wickedness

These racial justice concepts are the fruits of an ideology now spreading throughout our culture. I believe this framework appeals to people more for what they hope it can be rather than what it really is. They hope it is something good. They want it to be righteous. It calls itself by names that sound like positive ideals. People are attracted by the promised ideal, and so they are drawn in by their good intentions. Unfortunately, the positive feelings—and even hope—are overshadowed by attitudes of divisiveness and learned negativity.

I view much of the ideology as wicked because I do not know a better way to describe the zealotry that it breeds. It is wicked to pit people against each other based on skin color or other characteristics. This is not a healing practice of inclusion. It is division practiced in the name of inclusion. There must be a way to include all and to celebrate diversity without creating factions opposed to each other.

It is wicked to separate employees according to skin color or similar traits and teach them that one group is specifically and inherently racist while other groups can never be bigoted. One book became popular for teaching that white people who reject the notion that they are born racists are simply displaying fragility. I have heard from a few other friends who have been ushered into trainings on this concept. One reported that he was told to apologize for his inherent racism. Another shared that she was told that she as a white person is socialized to oppress.

It is especially wicked to bring this divisiveness to young children. Yet that is precisely what is happening in many schools. Christopher Rufo (*www.christopherrufo. com*) has written several articles describing exercises where elementary school children are taught to identify each other by skin color and section themselves off into "ranked" groups of greater to lesser power or oppression. The scenarios he shares include heart-breaking examples of little children being taught to hate and fear other groups of people. This is racism. And it is wicked.

There are hurts and pains associated with racial disparities. There are historical, political, institutional, family, and cultural realities that intersect to create real issues that affect real people. I do not trivialize these realities. On the contrary, I contend that these topics deserve greater service and sincerity than what is coming from the current antiracism ideology. The issues that drive interest in these conversations are complex. Principles, however, are not complicated. Let me share a little about what I mean by that.

I will start with what a retired military friend of mine would call the bottom-line up front (BLUF). The ideology driving the current antiracism (also called racial justice or racial equity) movement is a thought framework known as Critical Race Theory (CRT). This framework leads to what I believe is wickedness because it is designed to deconstruct and tear down. It focuses on conflict and emphasizes a continual struggle for power between groups.

It seeks out the study of conflict, not collaboration or unity. That is the bottom line for me—it is a framework that produces fruits of divisiveness, hatred and negativity. It is leaving car crash debris in our schools, places of work, houses of worship, and public squares.

There is a quote from one of the antiracist movement's thought leaders that provides a revealing summary. In his book, *How to be an Antiracist*, Ibram X. Kendi wrote: "The only remedy to racist discrimination is antiracist discrimination. The only remedy to past discrimination is present discrimination. The only remedy to present discrimination is future discrimination."As a Christian, in principle, I cannot support that statement. This seems like an argument for justifying retaliatory behavior. I see this a borderline vengeful. It is not my intention to place too much weight on a singular quote. His is not the only voice in the racial justice or antiracism movement. The quote offers a good example to explain how these complex issues can be less overwhelming if we focus on our principles first.

I hold to principles of fairness and equality, and I believe in treating people fairly and equally. These principles prevent me from supporting a notion that because something negative was done to a group of people in the past, then something negative should done to a different group of people now. This framework would also cause me to contradict a principle for honesty. It seems like a dishonest action to penalize a group of people in the present for something that occurred in previous generations. Already I have thought of three principles I would have to compromise to believe in his premise and agree with his approach. I will look instead for a better solution to support.

It is not loving to call for discrimination, or to teach people to show partiality toward others. This is basic dignity. It simply is not more complicated than that. Changing definitions of words or shifting discriminatory behavior toward other groups will not change the basic truth. Racism is prejudice or discrimination. It is sinful. And people of any color can be racist. To say otherwise is misguided.

This brings me to another aspect of wickedness that stems from the current antiracism philosophy. It not only assumes that people of color are somehow victims in society, but also encourages people to see victimhood in their experiences and circumstances. This eliminates hope and reduces self-empowerment. Even more harmful, it often teaches people to retaliate in direct and damaging ways.

To see an example, we need look no further than protests that devolve into rioting and looting. Defacing property, fighting in the streets, and stealing from stores is not justice or activism for a cause. It is criminal behavior and violence. I think most people understand that.

But there are also other instances where people have felt justified and have been encouraged to cause lasting harm to others in retaliation for their perceived experiences. What happened to a janitor at Smith College is a sad example. A student at the small, private college entered a lounge that was closed to the public and sat to eat lunch. Employees had been informed by campus police that the lounge was closed to anyone not involved with a summer camp group using the facility. Because background checks were necessary for all people working with the kids, campus police asked to be notified if anyone entered the closed lounge so that they could handle it themselves. A janitor saw the student there and reported it.

The student took offense and blasted the janitor on her social media posts as racist. She also posted that America is a scary place for black people. As a result, the college president put the employee on leave and immediately apologized to the student. The punch line is that a later investigation found the racism charge to be unfounded. In other words, people's lives were disrupted without question and without merit. (Powell, 2021)

I consider this a sad example because it paints a picture of how power and anger and resentment are often the leading outcomes of actions driven by this ideology. It is sad, and even a bit frightening, that the janitor was so easily disregarded. The person with the power and privilege in that situation was the student. Yet she chose to characterize herself as a victim for the purpose of retaliation and power over her perceived enemy. I'm not sure who is harmed more in these types of scenarios. One person was bitter and outraged while the other was penalized for following instructions and was defenseless against the student's bias.

What good comes from ideology that labels people and encourages conflict between groups of people? For Christians, what does scripture teach us about partiality and race?

Seeking Biblical Guidance to Follow Goodness over Wickedness

Racism is wicked. This does not require explanation. As I indicated earlier, I believe most Americans agree. It is our desire to eradicate racism, I believe, that fuels support for Critical Race Theory and the antiracism movement. The problem is, as I see it, that much of what is taught in Critical Race Theory is racism. There are many good sources to learn more about these movements and the ideology behind it. In a nutshell, CRT is an offshoot of Critical Theory. Critical Theory is an academic framework to critique society and to notice and challenge power structures. The presumption of power structures and struggles is baked into the cake, as they say.

Critical Theory got the presumption of power struggle from its parent philosophy, Marxism. Whereas Marxism was focused on the power struggles between economic classes, Critical Theory shifts the focus to seeing power struggles between cultural groups. CRT then shifts the focus to race and thus sees all of culture through a lens of noticing the power struggle between races. It does not question whether racism is present; it starts with a presumption that racism is always present. The questions then become how racism is manifesting and how to shift the balance of power to favor a different group. This brings me back to Kendi's quote on discrimination. He does not advocate to reduce it; his quote states that we must shift who is discriminated against.

How does the Bible guide us in navigating these concepts? For starters, let us focus again on the question of partiality. Partiality is how the Bible addresses what we know as racism. Remember, in our Christian worldview, there is only one race. We have differences in skin color and cultural heritage; but we are not actually different races. The Bible does not speak in terms of race, and the ancient world didn't either. For centuries people identified their various groups as different tribes or nations, but not as different races. The idea of race is a somewhat modern concept.

Partiality is one way to review how the Bible directs us to think about these matters. To show partiality means to favor one over another. Scripture tells us that God shows no partiality (Romans 2:11). What this means is that He does not favor groups of people—such as poor people or rich people or black people or white people—over other groups of people. God measures us against a moral and holy standard, not against each other. A tall person is not better than a short person, nor does God judge us according to our external features or appearances.

Thinking in these terms, that God shows no partiality, consider how beautiful the message is in 1 Samuel 16:7: But the Lord said to Samuel, "Do not consider his appearance or his height, for I have rejected him. The Lord does not look at the things people look at. People look at the outward appearance, but the Lord looks at the heart."

Because God's character is such that He shows no partiality, He also demands the same of us. As Christ's followers, we simply should not be in the habit of showing favoritism of one group (or individual) over another. Consider Leviticus 19:15: In teaching His people how to conduct justice, God commanded, "Do not pervert justice, do not show partiality to the poor or favoritism to the great, but judge your neighbor fairly."

James 2:9 tells us clearly: "But if you show partiality, you are committing sin. . . ."

These instructions are clear. Partiality is sin. In our terms, this means racism is sin. So too is an ideology that permits the sin of racism to be committed by one group that considers itself justified in doing so because it views another group as its oppressor. Partiality is partiality. And it is wrong.

I really do not have to get deeper than understanding how God feels about partiality to understand that it is wicked to promote antiracism and CRT. These ideologies intentionally promote partiality, which contradicts God's holy standard. Is that not the very essence of what wickedness is?

Every person, of every color and nationality, is made in the Imago Dei (the image of God). For this reason alone, we must treat every person with dignity. And because God demands justice, He calls us to treat every person fairly and without partiality. I believe this is true even if those people tell us they deserve favoritism because of past transgressions. I have not found these exception clauses in Scripture. We can do better than trading racism for racism. We can instead treat everyone—not just groups but individuals—with dignity and respect.

A biblical worldview gives us a right view of justice and sin. In CRT and the antiracism movement there is a clear absence of biblical understandings of justice, relationships to each other, reconciliation, sin, and even love. Ibram X. Kendi seemed to highlight this very thing when he talked about his theology at a recent appearance. In describing that he believes in liberation theology, he said that "savior theology" "… goes right in line with racist ideals and racist theology." (Dreher, March 2021)

Kendi, under his worldview of viewing the world as a continual power struggle of the classes, favors a liberation theology based on salvation through revolution of the classes. Different worldviews drive cultural, political, philosophical and even academic views. As I share next, our worldviews also influence behaviors and attitudes.

CHAPTER SEVEN

LIVE FREE
AND FAITHFUL

Other Worldviews

At one of my early college jobs, I worked at a small ice cream and dessert shop. Because I worked nearly full-time, I was there almost every day and became friends with everyone on the crew. We were a small team—we all had different backgrounds and aspirations for life. It was an adventure for, just getting to know each of these friends. I was "fresh off the farm" and had grown up in a much more sheltered environment than they had. They each teased me a good bit because they considered me less exposed and worldly than they, but it was all in good fun. We were a motley crew—and we liked that.

I remember each of them for various reasons, probably because it was enjoyable to be around so many different lifestyles for the first time. The one who comes to mind now is Duane. He was about three years older than I and close to graduating in something from the physical sciences (subject areas I had little in-terest in at the time). He was intelligent, outgoing and considerably more assertive than I about expressing his beliefs. I remember this because he was an atheist, and once he learned that I was Christian, he sought regular debates and opportunities to challenge me on my worldview.

Here's the thing: At that time all I really meant when I said I was Christian was that I believed in God. I didn't have a whole lot of substance or conviction beyond that. But I have always been pretty open about talking with others and I was up for the same with him. I was curious about where he was coming from and why he believed what he did. Admittedly, I was no match for him in terms of conviction or even depth of my beliefs back then. Still, he never convinced me on his worldview, even though he seemed to be trying to do just that.

I think that is what I remember most about our conversations. He mocked my views a good bit—and rightly mocked my lack of knowledge on those views. He chided me a good bit by insisting that atheism is much more intelligent as a worldview. That seemed to be an important message for him. It also seemed important for him to be able to make me see things his way. Yet, even though I could not match his depth, I still found most of his arguments to be unpersuasive.

I didn't understand why he tried so hard to convince me. It was the first time I had been openly "witnessed" to become more secular and turn away from belief. But it was not the last. There was one professor who told me that belief in God is naïve, and another who told me that college students should know that all gods are myths. Along the way, there have also been several friends who have attempted to encourage me toward different lifestyles, beliefs, or religious affiliation.

My point is that since I have not been a Christian all my life, I am aware that it's not only Christians who proselytize. I have been personally invited to become a believer of Atheism, Buddhism, New Age/New Thought, Universalism, Feminism, and Progressivism. There have also been many customs and preferences that I've been personally invited to agree with or disagree (i.e., drinking, not drinking, gay marriage, legalized marijuana). People with beliefs about how to live tend to share those beliefs. This is not exclusive to Christians.

In current culture, I think you would agree that this tendency has become magnified. All four corners of culture seem to have preachers promoting the importance of believing one way or another. It seems to have gone beyond persuasion and sharing ideas. Look and listen. I am sure you'll hear people trying to pull you into one belief system or another.

I share this because I sense a reticence among many fellow Christians to speak up for our beliefs, often for fear of seeming "preachy" or "pushy." This resonates with me too. I've not been one to share my faith with others without first evaluating how receptive they may be. This is true even now, that I have grown in my faith and now have a personal relationship with Jesus. It is still ingrained in me not to push faith. Duane did not have that hesitation. He may not have called it such, but he witnessed his religion to me on more than one occasion.

No. Despite how uncomfortable we may feel about sharing our faith and beliefs openly, it is not true that only people of faith preach. I am sure you too have sensed a religious zeal around many of the political and cultural issues moving in society right now. You know that adage –if it looks like a duck, swims like a duck, and quacks like a duck? Well….

There is a reason much of the promoting and persuading from advocates and activists feels like proselytizing. I mean, come on, these movements seem to require adoption of certain beliefs AND customs AND opinions. It is expected that followers comply with these behaviors and follow only accepted leaders. Want an example? How about a few?

Proponents and trainers of the CRT movement promote advice that people of a certain skin color should "take up less space," while also advising that people of another skin color have a special insight called "lived experience" that takes precedence over any contradictory facts. There is also repetitive reference to a collective original sin and a demand for repentance. What's missing is any hope of redemption or reconciliation. This is not a religion of relationship, but rather power.

It is my opinion that, for some, political activism has indeed become a sort of religion. We are all made to worship, as a person of faith you would probably agree that we all worship something. Add to that a growing loss of meaning for many in society, it makes sense that the search for places to find such meaning would include politics. For me, before I came to Jesus, it was career. That was where I thought I would find most of the purpose in my life. I was wrong.

Yes. There is a religious fervor—and sometimes a canon of required beliefs—behind some of our current cultural topics. Searching for meaning explains many of the followers. I also caution that this is not the only explanation. Political movements have believers. They also have leaders and thought leaders who design the political framework. Those people, the ones with the agenda, have a direction they want the thing to go.

Our founders, for example, steered us in a direction of independence, equal opportunity, and balanced, limited government power. Not every framework drives in the same direction. Nor does every ideology come from the same set of beliefs or worldview. And the foundational worldview, my friend, has a lot to do with which direction movements are headed—and what values and principles will be supported along the way.

A Word about Worldview Building Blocks

This section is not an argument for Republican or Democrat. I am a Republican. You don't have to be for us to have common ground. That was an underlying point I hope I conveyed in chapter two. Our common ground as Americans is not a political party or skin color; but is our shared creed. We are citizens of a nation unique in the fact that it is founded by creed. These ideas are what determines how we order our society.

As believers, however, we also have an underlying worldview that holds even higher ground in our minds and hearts. We share, for example, a common understanding that there is a God and that He is the Creator of the universe. I believe our Founding Fathers shared that worldview.

Not everyone believes in a created world. Have you ever thought about how that simple belief difference most assuredly influences everything else about the worldviews we develop? This is the basic building block. Paul told us as much, didn't he? In Romans 1:19-20 he said that it is plain for everyone to see that God exists. Then in Romans 1:21-25 he went on to say that those who denied God became fools and worshiped creation rather than the Creator.

I agree with theologian and author Peter Jones in his book, *The Other Worldview – Exposing Christianity's Greatest Threat.* Jones wrote that in this passage from Paul, we learn that there are two basic worldviews: Either we worship the Creator, or we worship creation (Jones, 2015, p. 11). Our basic belief, whether we believe in a moral God who made the world or in a self-generating world, will inform quite a lot about how we interpret everything we learn.

Of course, paganism comes to mind, conjuring images of sacrificing lives to appease various forces of nature. What about more modern examples? I'll get there. First let me stop by a few other places in history—like the French Revolution.

The French Revolution of 1789 contrasts the American Revolution in several ways. Our revolution resulted in a founding based on the ideas on inherent equality of all people, an understanding that there is a higher moral power, and a relatively free economy. The French Revolution resulted in anarchy which then led to dictatorship. (Peterson, 1989).

By the early 1790s there was anarchy from radical insurgents and ongoing massacres, followed by a guillotined king. Then radical Jacobin socialists took over government, outlawed Christianity, and began the Reign of Terror that beheaded thousands (History. com, 2021).

Then came a weakened attempt at government followed by the rise of a dictator. Though goals about freedom of speech and equality were a part of the revolution's story, centralized power, mass beheadings and socialist land seizure became the characteristics we remember. And what of the goals to outlaw and eradicate Christianity? Yes. There had been church and monarchy entanglement and abuse, but I would argue that a political movement to eradicate Christianity alto-gether is not a reaction to abuses but rather is evidence of a particular kind of worldview.

Karl Marx, a socialist from a later era, may give us a hint. He is famous for having said "religion is the opiate of the masses." He saw religion as only neces-sary when a society is not well-ordered. In contrast, he believed that if a society becomes rightly ordered, then the desire for faith would disappear. (Jones, p. 20).

Marx is arguably the most well-known socialist thought leader. He is worth mentioning in this book because of my earlier chapter on the anti-racism move-ment fueled by CRT (a framework that gets its roots in Critical Theory and, ultimately, Marxist thought). Marx desired creating utopian society of sorts through class warfare. He viewed society as a conflict over power between classes of people, and that the solution was a revolution where the working class would seize pro-duction and build a socialist society.

His dream of class warfare revolution has, in my opinion, landed in our culture as an attempt to flame racial wars. These ideologies have been forming since the 1960s, with names you may remember like the Black Panthers and the Weather Underground (Rufo, June 2021).

By the 1990's, the ideology resurfaced as Critical Race Theory. It often goes under other names like equity, social justice, diversity and inclusion, and culturally responsive teaching (Rufo, June, 2021). Stoking racial strife, by any name, is not a recipe for bringing about a morally decent society.

Marx's idea of a man-made utopia was founded through a different worldview than what matches my principles. He was an atheist, and as such, believed that the material world is all there is. Influenced by the popular humanist movement of his era, he seemed also to believe that by his reason alone, man can create a perfectly ordered society.

There is a lot for me to be skeptical about in that worldview. History has shown us that the same ambition that drives this belief (that man can and should order society with tight control)—well it usually turns into the same type of ambition that ends in control and death of the masses. Think about our various collectivist movements that arose under the guise of advancing social justice in one way or another. In their wake are more than 100 million dead—mass starvation, massacres, genocide, eugenics, and collapsed economies.

In worshiping the creation, man may think he can create a perfectly ordered society. The rub may lie in what a materialist worldview holder sees as perfectly ordered. One where only certain types of people have value? One where you have no agency to better yourself or your family economically? One where you are stripped of property and dignity? A society that is ordered outside of God's moral standards—or in contradiction to them—will ultimately lead to societal trauma.

Morals and Principles

Part of what goes on with other worldviews is divided morality. It is not that people with different worldviews don't want morality in society. Everyone has a moral compass of some kind, for we are given a conscience. Yet without a worldview shaped by God's revelation about his holy character and morality, then people are left with the probability of misunderstanding moral laws.

It is not easy, as I'm sure you've noticed, to override emotions and preferences in favor of morality. Unbelievers have less protection against falling prey to subjective morality, or even relativism. Believers too, must beware. When we don't see the standard— or the plumb line—we can also fall prey to counterfeit morals imposed by mob mentality or public bullying.

An example, once again, is in the antiracism movement. Racist trainings that overtly categorize and stereotype people are not morally righteous. I know the framework and the issue is more complicated than this one sentence. Remember—while issues may be complex, principles are simple.

That is how I believe you can sus out where you stand on these complex issues. Do not react by emotion or crowd think. Choose instead to respond by principle. How does it match up to or contradict your core worldview? It is not that you can't then believe something if it contradicted your basic worldview. You should, however, examine if it has a weight worthy of shifting your principles.

Your worldview and principles inform how you interpret the world around you. We gather knowledge and evaluate what we learn based on what we already know or in comparison to different types of knowledge we can access. The worldview will especially influence the presumptions we start with and the conclusions we draw about what we learn.

For example, the critical theorists apparently bring the presumption that human relationships are viewed in terms of power struggles between groups of people. They seem to then conclude that shifting power is what is required for relationship healing of any kind. As Christians, you and I should share a different presumption that we are all on the same plane as sinners before a Holy God. Our concluding resolution is not shifting power, but rather accepting the grace of our Lord and righting our relationship with God so that as a result we can live a right and loving relationship with others.

The truth is that choosing a different worldview than that of a believer— this is the decisive choice laid before us for all time. What we choose, to believe and love God or not, is the ultimate individual choice. As for our society and culture—moral law still exists. Defying those standards is sin against God, and it will invite chaos.

Freedom or Tyranny

My alarm bell is this: There is chaos knocking at our door. Have you heard its echoes yet? I have only scratched the surface when it comes to talking about confusing and chaotic issues for our culture. Where do you think the current cultural and political movements will take our society?

I do not know the answer either, of course, but I have my concerns. I see some patterns in the world-views like those that inform study of conflict theory, treating justice as a game of group power, stereotyping people according to various groups, and centralizing power for controlling the masses and suppressing divergent opinions.

I also see parallels to other moments in history. I cannot be the only one who sees a relationship between stereotyping white people or black people to past propaganda efforts to dehumanize other groups. There must be other people who see a parallel in promoting extreme preferential treatment in the name of achieving equal outcomes to the failed redistributive policies that create economic devastation.

The question knocking at the door is whether we are in danger of shifting away from freedom toward tyranny. Lest you reject the notion because tyranny sounds far-fetched due to absence of monarchy in our system, understand all the ways tyranny has and can take root.

I think it is fair to characterize tyranny as absolute power, or oppressive control. Now let me say this a slightly different way, absolute power or control unrestrained by law. We associate this with cruel, authoritarian dictators in history. However, tyranny is not only implemented by a singular tyrant or dictator.

Another word like tyranny, for example, is totalitarianism. In his book, *Live Not by Lies,* Rod Dreher summarizes this as a "state in which nothing can be permitted to exist that contradicts a society's ruling ideology." (Dreher, p. 30). Totalitarian tyranny states have (and do) exist in forms like communism and fascism.

It is also worth mentioning oligarchies, in which groups (families, businesses, etc.) rule. Why are these relevant? Well, think beyond government structure for a moment and consider the various power structures that have expanding control in our society right now.

Think about our social media public squares as an example. We have tech giant companies here benefitting legally from a legal protection against liabilities of publisher responsibility for content, based on a presumed status as being not publishers but mere hosts of online information (much like phone lines). Armed with this protection, these platforms have become arbiters of what can and cannot be published.

This may seem too small for concern in your mind. I refer you to principle-based thinking. Is it in our best interest as a free society that monopoly tech giants can seemingly collude with political leaders to remove dissent or alternate opinions from the public square?

In the past year they have restricted information about virus treatment from doctors—treatment now revealed to be a viable treatment that saves lives. They have removed a former president, which may or may not be pleasing to you because his messages were often annoying. Yet I cannot help but think of it this way: If a sitting president and former president can be censored in that way, what chance does a regular citizen have against their absolute power?

Speaking of power, the pandemic year revealed a readiness in many state and local governments to all but completely control its citizens' movements, economic freedom, and religious freedom. Whether it truly began as necessary at the level it was implemented is arguable. What is not arguable is that freedoms were restricted and applied unequally—states that banned public gatherings openly supported gatherings for protests and riots. Absolute power? Arbitrary application of control?

This brings me back to the issues I have discussed in this book: equity, social justice, and antiracism. Here is my question for you, dear reader. Do you believe you have freedom in this culture to openly speak about your positions or opinions on these topics? Do you feel free to discuss your opinions online or in public without fear of attack or suppression?

How about related to issues of gender confusion and various sexuality topics, even among kids? Do you feel as though our current culture will accept counter viewpoints on these subjects? Can you express your views, or even basic biological facts, about these topics in the public square, or even your place of work, without concern for retribution?

Perhaps you feel comfortable with all of it and trust that there is no suppression of speech or opinion. If so, I hope you are correct. If our culture cowers back and allows tyranny through mob mentality or oligarchical power from tech companies, it can be just as oppressive as totalitarian government policies.

Freedom is not an easy thing to maintain. Individuals readily want autonomy, if they view it as their license to make their own way and fulfil their own desires. For this type of godlike power, people will even fight. You have heard it with phrases like "my body, my choice" as a mantra to simultaneously hold oneself literally unaccountable for previous choices while claiming absolute right to take another life.

When autonomy drivers reach these levels in society, freedom may weirdly be at risk—because people are concerned with self so much that they are willing to suppress the liberties of others. Add collectivist mentalities of dehumanizing individuals as nothing more than parts of a group; and then society can develop totalitarian and tyrannical viewpoints about how they relate to fellow citizens.

From where do these harsh viewpoints originate? I believe they are formed at the basic level from a materialistic worldview, an attachment to this world as all that there is. It is from this worldview that comes a willingness to classify people by worth, rank groups of people, and even eliminate or prevent people through "planning" policies.

When people become little more than elements of a group, or little symbols of the physical characteristics they display, then things can get cold and controlling. These collectivist attitudes are anathema to a biblical understanding of the dignity of each person. These attitudes also stem from views that government holds godlike authority and privilege to engineer society and control people's lives (with force as needed).

Freedom and liberty stem from a different worldview: God is in control and governmental leaders are responsible to God just as citizens are. Freedom also requires obedience, an understanding that there is a moral lawgiver to whom we all are accountable. Finally, freedom demands self-regulation and personal responsibility—in a free society we cannot succumb to every passion and desire, and we cannot demand endless benefits from our government.

Freedom—and faith--also call for courage. It takes courage to speak up for freedom over totalitarian movements, ideologies, cultural dogmas, and political policies. It also takes courage to speak up for values and principles in a culture leaning into confusion and licentiousness. Whether it is in personal conversations or in public forums, we must find our clarity and speak light where we have influence.

We are called to freedom. We are called to faith. And we are called to courage.

CHAPTER EIGHT

SPEAK BOLDLY

How to find courage

It took me some time to find the courage to write this book. I have been thinking about and discussing these topics with my friends for more than a year. As I wrote in the first chapter, talking politics comes to me naturally and comfortably. My mind rarely thirsts for opinions either. Courage did not elude me for any lack of interest or clear thoughts on the related subject matter.

The writing itself is not where my courage struggled. There are the usual barriers—thoughts about whether people will enjoy reading it and whether my writing can maintain interest in long form. Overcoming these types of limiting thoughts, however, still did not take that much courage. Like other writers before me, the words simply had to be released.

A book is a different matter. Putting my thoughts here is more of a leap. I enjoy this opportunity to share with you these stories and ideas. This required me to first summon my courage. Books are tangible. They last. These are the very things I like about them.

Yet there was still a hesitation, perhaps even a fear, that lurked in my mind's recesses even as the words flowed freely. It was not readily obvious to me why—or even that it was there. It just sort of wrapped around me in that steady way fear has when it surfaces just enough to keep us in our comfort zone. It is quite possible that had I not stopped for reflection I may not have even become fully aware I had any fear. Ignoring it though, is not the best way to overcome it.

That is my first tip about finding your courage. Awareness is the first step. A solid understanding of your current reality, as well as your expectations and desires. This awareness, a broader perspective and deeper insight, is the first step in my three-step coach approach (Size Up/Shore Up/Step Up). It makes sense to me, then, that the first step to finding your courage is recognizing your fear.

Don't stop at recognition. Look at the fear. Size it up. Name it. Search out why it's there and what it is. Ask yourself what it is that you fear. What is the worst that can happen? Consider what you have to lose, or what you might gain. I imagine fear to be like conflict in this way: Ignoring it and leaving it in a dark corner allows it to grow, while sunlight makes it dissipate.

The first step, understanding, helped me. I was not afraid of publishing a book in general. You, reader, are also not in my fear zone, I suspect. For if you have read this far, we must share a good bit of common ground on these issues. Or you are the sort of person who enjoys diverse opinions without angst or offense.

That was my fear, I believe. I was unknowingly a part of the 60% I mentioned in my introduction, who are afraid of expressing political opinions that may upset other people. I did not know it right away because in my small circles I don't seem to feel fear in that way.

I suppose that is because I can interact in real time and give assurances about my intent and tone.

A book is different. But I needed to write it. I believe in its message. We are free citizens, not subjects. We have a heritage of flourishing and overcoming, not oppression. We can examine our whole history without creating hate and shame among each other. And we must value people and dignity, and share attitudes of joy, opportunity, and gratitude. These are elements of light—and they will serve our culture and our posterity much, much better than division and bitter causes of power plays.

Your courage is in your purpose, wrapped in your values and principles and the things that matter for eternity. Look there. That's where you'll find it.

We Must Engage as Local, Courageous Citizens

Citizenship is not a spectator sport. As citizens of a free country, each of us likes to say we have rights and freedoms. We also have duty and responsibility. These are less enjoyed aspects. Usually not because we don't want to engage, but because it often seems overwhelming to figure out where we can have impact. Our government has become large and unwieldy. I suspect most of us realize this during the times we would like to influence change. It can be difficult to imagine turning the wheel or tapping the brake in such a large engine as our national bureaucratic and political system.

It frankly is with this national behemoth that leftist-oriented movements have an advantage over centrists, moderates and conservatives. These are often the same people who support centralized power and a large, administrative state. This seems to make them more prone to develop national messages and movements that appear to operate in lockstep. As we see in our current culture, the left has also gravitated toward demanding solidarity on opinions and thought and public discourse.

The extreme left and the extreme right, as far as I am concerned, tend to meet in the same place in the end—abuse of power and oppressive control. It is the extreme left, however, that has worrisome traction today. And they have been playing a systematic long game since the days of Wilson or before to chip away at free markets, free religion, property rights, equality, and more. So much so, that it is, frankly, an extremely difficult task to counter the mass messaging and national political or cultural debates. They call it Progressivism, but I don't think they are progressing toward what the average American supports.

The good news is that our strengths as individual citizens lie elsewhere. As does our impact. It is still true that all politics are local. And local is where you can have the most influence and the most open access to your government representation. Local is also where you live—it is where both culture and politics impact you most directly. Local is where you engage.

Local citizenship is the natural counterweight against collectivist and totalitarian movements. It does not feel like it is big enough to make a dent. Yet it is probably the only thing that can. After all, our Constitution was made to bind together several states, not build a central command. Freedom and equality thrive in communities of people and neighbors, not masses of strangers and stereotyped groups.

To reduce overwhelm, localize by issue as well as geography. There are too many topics roiling to follow them all effectively. I have chosen to discuss topics I find particularly troubling because of the division, broken relationships, and possibly even divided churches I believe they will cause. Yet I know there are many other issues that may catch more of your attention.

Follow where you have interest and where your courage will allow you to influence and educate. Choose your interests—but I encourage a sense of responsibility toward at least one of the culturally dividing issues. It is not about getting into debates. Your courage is for helping people think more clearly and speak common sense into a culture of confusion. That is what this is all about. I believe more of us must step up in the ways that we can.

Where We Must Stand

Deceptive politics and wicked movements are spreading in our local spheres of influence. It is hitting home, as the saying goes. Here are some of the places where I believe we must find the courage to speak into immediately and regularly.

State Legislatures and City Councils: I know these spheres are potentially boring for many, and I understand. However, we are in a season when these bodies may be adopting policies that you don't expect. Here is a potential example. The current presidential administration is discussing ideas like state and local pressure or grants to influence local residential zoning.

Local zoning should first consider local citizens. Know when your council meets. Perhaps attend a meeting or two. Go online and review past meeting minutes.

Conversely, local or state bodies may not be acting on something you believe they could. For example, several state legislatures are discussing legislation on topics like racism in public school curriculum. Is your state? Do you want to take part? Find your legislature online and review the committee schedule (look for local government, education, finance, etc.). On many sites you can either watch a televised committee or sign up for email alerts on bills in certain committees or on certain topics. Don't rely on local news. Choose your focus and gather knowledge.

Schools: I cannot emphasize this enough. If you have children in K-12 schools, make this your first stop. Know what they are learning. Seriously. If you are not yet aware of what could be taking place, research Cupertino Elementary School in California or Dalton School in Manhattan. Look for stories on parent pushback in Loudoun County, Virginia; and research Eastside Manhattan School and the 8 White Identities. Our children are being trained as activists. Remember parents, these children and their moral upbringing are gifts and responsibilities charged to you from God Himself. They are not subjects of the state to be trained in its favored ideology. You have every right to know what they are learning and to speak up about what you find.

There are a few organizations providing research and support to help you identify whether your school is peddling racist theories. I will share a couple links here, but I urge you first to go directly to your school as well. Discern what you are told. I don't expect that every teacher or school board member knows what they are promoting. You can speak in plain terms with them, though, and express your expectations for quality education.

Here are a few resources to help you research:

- Parents Defending Education: *www.defending-ed.org*

- Foundation Against Intolerance and Racism: *www.fairforall.org*

- City Journal Articles on Radical Teachings in Schools: *https://www.city-journal.org/contributor/christopher-f-rufo_1334*

Churches: The most important point I want to convey about churches is to be aware of any false gospel. I have already shared that I believe CRT contradicts biblical justice. It counters the gospel in these important ways: It excuses the sin of racism on the one hand by naming it as systemic and calling for a repentance to a people group instead of to God. Many of these antiracism training groups, including one that was at one point invited to my local church, promote that whiteness is a sin and that apparently one from which one can find no redemption. How does this align with the true gospel that says Jesus is sufficient, and that when we come to him, we put aside all other identities and are family unified in Christ?

I have been surprised to see this teaching take root in churches so easily. I understand the impulse, but I don't understand the need for a church to reach beyond the gospel. Yet I suspect this is a place where these issues will arise innocently and without understanding of the ideology. The only thing I can recommend here is to listen with discernment and ask questions when warranted. Explore the issue together and stay grounded in biblical text. God really has provided all the guidance we need to treat one another with dignity and love. I see it this way: It is to God that we are to reconcile, and in so doing, everyone in the family is reconciled through Christ.

I have one final resource to offer in relation to churches. If your church considers doing one of these antiracism trainings or struggle sessions, there is an organization I recommend promoting for consideration. The Center for Biblical Unity (*www.centerforbiblicalunity*) creates content and trainings for the faith community to approach racism and reconciliation under a biblical worldview.

These local centers—state legislatures, city councils, schools and school boards, and churches--are the core areas where we must stand up and speak up. We cannot remain idle as damaging lies are infecting our communities and families. Uncomfortable as it may be to ask questions and challenge assumptions, this is one of those moments in history when we must find the courage. When only a few people speak up, it is construed as dissent. When most of us speak up, it is a conversation. Let's bring conversation—and clear thinking and common sense—back to our public squares.

PARTING WORDS

This is a clarion call. I hope you hear it. It is not a call for grievance activism, or shouting, or creating more division by belittling others. Our call is something different. We challenge assumptions and damaging ideas. It is the lies that we condemn, not the people.

We are the tolerant, for we are the ones who can listen to divergent opinions. We are the compassionate, because we understand treating people with dignity and love is much more authentic than simple affirmation of all the choices they make. We are genuine because we study both the beauty and ugliness of our past without losing our perspective of our ideals.

It is truth that we seek to find and share. We cannot be silent while radicals wreak undue influence on our culture. We must find the courage to stand up and speak up—for our heritage, our values, and better judgment. Salt and Light.

Woe to those who call evil good and good evil,
who put darkness for light and light for darkness,
who put bitter for sweet and sweet for bitter.
- Isaiah 5:20

ABOUT THE AUTHOR

Vicki Rich is a coach and consultant who works with people to reach their next level of aptitude and fulfillment. She has a passion for helping them take charge of what they can control and empower themselves to reach new levels of impact and significance in their lives. She believes the best goals in life are not about self—but about making a greater difference or giving valuable service to the world. Happiness does not come merely from seeking happiness itself. Happiness comes from a result of living a life of virtue, contribution, love, and impact.

Her two guiding views in coaching are: 1.) each person is able (if willing) to create desired changes; and 2.) the process of change requires understanding, responsibility, and action. Her coaching model is summarized as: Size Up, Shore Up and Step Up. It's a method she uses to help people simplify their situation, identify the resources they need to change their situation, and take actions toward what they want or how they can make a greater impact.

Vicki enjoys learning the patterns that connect disparate concepts and breaking down complex information into simple terms. Clients experience a greater sense of calmness and ability to cut through overwhelm more easily as a result of working with Vicki. Colleagues have also shared that she helped them capture their thoughts in a way that centered them and gave them greater focus.

Vicki is the author of a self-coaching book on empowering yourself to greater career confidence and satisfaction, also through clear thinking and self-awareness. She also works with and coaches aspiring authors and leaders who want to share their insight and stories through books or other content. To explore working with Vicki through coaching, sharing your story, or developing a strong message for your vision; contact her at *vicki@reachnextlevel.com*.

NOTES

Chapter Four

- Pink, Daniel. Drive. (2009). Riverhead Books. New York, New York. Pp. 83-106.

Chapter Five

- Brown, Lee. (Aug 21, 2020). NY Post. BLM organizer who called looting reparations dismisses peaceful protesting. *https://nypost.com/2020/08/13/blm-organizer-who-called-looting-reparations-doubles-down/*

- Dreher, Rod. (March 24, 2021). The American Conservative. Antiracist, Anti-Christian. *https://www.theamericanconservative.com/dreher/kendi-antiracist-antichristian-critical-race-theory/*

- Harris, Kamala. (Nov 1, 2020). Twitter. There's a big difference between equality and equity. Political Campaign Video. *https://twitter.com/KamalaHarris/status/1322963321994289154*

- Powell, Michael. (Feb 26, 2021). The New York Times. Liberal orthodoxy, race and power: How and accusation of racism, and resulting lack of evidence is riling Smith College. *How an accusation of racism, and resulting lack of evidence, is riling Smith College - Chicago Tribune. Inside a Battle Over Race, Class and Power at Smith College - The New York Times (nytimes.com)*

Chapter Seven

- Dreher, Rod. Live Not by Lies. (2020). Sentinel. New York, New York. Pp. 30-31

- History.Com, Editors. (Feb 4, 2021). French Revolution. *https://www.history.com/topics/france/french-revolution*

- Jones, Peter. (2015). The Other Worldview: Exposing Christianity's Greatest Threat. Kirkdale Press. Bellingham, WA.

- Peterson, Robert A. (1989). A tale of two revolutions. Foundation for Economic Education. Articles. *https://fee.org/articles/a-tale-of-two-revolutions/*

- Rufo, Christopher. (June 14, 2021). Critical Race Theory Film. *https://christopherrufo.com/critical-race-theory-film*

- Rufo, Christopher. (April 27, 2021). Critical Race Theory in Education. *https://christopherrufo.com/critical-race-theory-in-education/*

- Williamson, Thaddeus. Confronting Injustice without Compromising Truth.

Made in United States
Orlando, FL
16 November 2021

10470486R00066